LEVELS JOURNAL

&

WORKBOOK

LOVE

PAIN

PURPOSE

PEACE

By Felicia Nicole

Printed in the United States of America
ISBN 978-0-578-28107-0

Travelin' Light Publishing
Travelinlight.mg@gmail.com
Cover and Interior design by Travelin' Light Publishing

WELCOME

When you complete this Journal, I want you to have figured out that this is your time. Make peace and keep moving forward. You are meant to be where you are. You are deserving of wealth, good health and happiness. You are not an imposter. Don't fall into that line of thinking this is a mistake or a fluke. This is part of your life's path. Fully execute this to the fullest extent of your ability. Work through this. Make time for rest. Your life is worth the fulfillment of your dreams, sweat and planning. Start now; begin again, fail then try again. Do what you need to do for your greatness. IT'S LEVELS TO THIS!

-Nyasia Monique

BIRTHDAYS & ANNIVERSARIES

January

_____
_____
_____
_____
_____
_____
_____

February

_____
_____
_____
_____
_____
_____
_____

March

_____
_____
_____
_____
_____
_____
_____

April

_____
_____
_____
_____
_____
_____

May

_____
_____
_____
_____
_____
_____
_____

June

_____
_____
_____
_____
_____
_____
_____

July

_____
_____
_____
_____
_____
_____
_____

August

_____
_____
_____
_____
_____
_____
_____

September

_____
_____
_____
_____
_____
_____

October

_____
_____
_____
_____
_____
_____

November

_____
_____
_____
_____
_____

December

_____
_____
_____
_____
_____

Financial literacy is the key to success:

1. Set Boundaries
2. Set Financial Goals
3. Think strategically
4. Prepare for Emergencies

Use this calendar to create an extensive budget. Hold yourself accountable to your budget and go hard!

January	February	March	April

May	June	July	August

September	October	November	December

TO DO LIST

SHORT TERM GOAL

_____

_____

_____

_____

_____

_____

_____

_____

TO DO LIST

LONG TERM GOAL

MAKE YOUR GOALS BIGGER

THAN YOUR FEARS

NO OUTSIDE
VALIDATION
IS REQUIRED
LOOK ABOVE
AND SEARCH
WITHIN
YOU GOT THIS!

– Felicia Nicole

SEVEN THINGS YOU FEEL ARE BEAUTIFUL ABOUT YOU

1. _____

2. _____

3. _____

4. _____

5. _____

6. _____

7. _____

LET LOVING YOURSELF BE YOUR BIGGEST ACHEIVEMENT, THE ONE YOU VALUE THE MOST. I PROMISE AFTER LOVING YOURSELF CORRECTLY, YOU CAN CONQUER THE WORLD.

-Felicia Nicole

_____

_____

_____

_____

_____

_____

_____

_____

SEVEN THINGS ABOUT YOURSELF YOU WANT TO IMPROVE NOT CHANGE

1. _____

2. _____

3. _____

4. _____

5. _____

6. _____

7. _____

-IMPROVING DOESN'T MEAN BAD

-IMPROVING MEANS ELEVATING, LEVELING UP, YOU MY DEAR ARE AMAZING!

COMPLACENCY

Complacency: Noun

Learner's definition of COMPLACENCY

: A feeling of being satisfied with how things are and not wanting to try to make them better: a complacent feeling or condition.

A feeling of calm satisfaction with your own abilities or situation, that prevents you from trying harder.

Do not get comfortable with your own or someone else's complacency.

Complacency is the killer of dreams; it keeps you satisfied with the status quo.

You should never become satisfied with the status quo if you are trying to be successful.

Your team and circle of people all must have the same mindset.

You have to get out there, work hard and not be afraid to fail.

Your journey to success is like a raft. If there is someone on your raft drilling holes, patch the holes and throw them off the raft. You will not and cannot reach the next level if you have a complacent heart and hole drillers.

-Felicia Nicole

They'll be people who will paint their picture of you! Remember their perception of you is NOT your responsibility! What YOU think and how YOU perceive yourself is your responsibility.

-Felicia Nicole

_____

_____

_____

_____

_____

_____

_____

SEVEN PLACES YOU WANT TO SEE, ANY PLACE IN THE WORLD

_____

1. _____

2. _____

3. _____

4. _____

5. _____

6. _____

7. _____

-MAKE IT HAPPEN, TAKE THE TRIP, YOU DESERVE THE TRIP

DARKEST FEARS PAGE

FAITH

OVER

FEAR

AS LONG AS
YOU TRY YOUR BEST
YOU'RE WINNING!

SECRETS PAGE

YOUR EYES ONLY

_____

_____

_____

_____

_____

_____

_____

THIS PAGE IS FOR YOU TO WRITE DOWN WHAT/WHO HAS HURT YOU THE MOST IN YOUR LIFE, THEN BURN IT. THIS IS TO SYMBOLISE LETTING GO OF THIS PAIN.

_____

_____

_____

_____

_____

_____

_____

BURNER PAGE TWO

_____

_____

_____

_____

_____

_____

_____

_____

-YOU CAN ONLY MOVE ON ONCE YOU'VE LET IT GO!!!

Breathe with intention, acknowledge what you are feeling in this very moment. But know that you are powerful and capable! Now release by exhaling every negative feeling and thought. Tell yourself I'm stronger than I know. Pick yourself up and Go!! Everything always feels worse than it really is! Keep Breathing! Keep Going! You Got This!!!

-Christine Smith

_____

_____

_____

_____

_____

_____

_____

Keep it moving, you will figure it out! If there's a wall, go around it or knock that bitch down!

-Michelle Polly Murriel

_____

_____

_____

_____

_____

_____

_____

_____

Do not be anxious about anything, but in every situation, by prayer and petition, with thanksgiving, present your requests to God. And the peace of God, which transcends all understanding, will guard your hearts and your minds in Christ Jesus.

Philippians 4:6–7 (NIV)

How did you interpret this scripture and how did it make you feel?

_____

_____

_____

_____

_____

_____

_____

"Have I not commanded you? Be strong and courageous. Do not be frightened, and do not be dismayed, for the LORD your God is with you wherever you go."
Joshua 1:9

How did you interpret this scripture and how did it make you feel?

_____

_____

_____

_____

_____

_____

_____

Humble yourselves, therefore, under the mighty hand of God so that at the proper time He may exalt you, casting all your anxieties on Him, because He cares for you.

1 Peter 5:6–7

How did you interpret this scripture and how did it make you feel?

_____

_____

_____

_____

_____

_____

_____

The Layers of Thick Clouds

Move beyond the Layers of Thick Clouds, past the grey skies, rain and gloomy days. Keep going! Past the layers of hurt, anger, guilt, blame and shame. Moving past those days where everything just stays the same. Keep going! Do you see the change? Can't you see the sun beaming in? Keep going past the Layers of Thick Clouds and meet the beautiful light that shines within.

-Melissa Sue Griffith

_____

_____

_____

_____

_____

_____

It's Your Turn Girl

You've encouraged everybody else, Girl!

You've stood in the stands

Clappin' your hands cheering them on
While they maaad dashed for the finish line
But you were next in line, Girl!
You gotta get in the race, Girl!

Jump in the rope, Girl!

It's your turn

It's your tun, now

It's your turn, Girl!

If I didn't know any better, I'd
think you'd rather bet on them than
believe in you No, Girl!
Time's a wasting, Girl!

Go girl, get on in the race, Girl!

It's your turn

It's your turn, now

It's your turn, Girl!

Run on while your legs are good and strong

Jump in the rope before discouragement demands that you quit!

Go on, Girl!

It's your turn

It's your turn, now

It's your turn, Girl!

©2021- Sharon Shaw

HEALING

Whatever we go through in life is a part of our growth. I don't care what it is! I believe that the intentions of what we may have experienced in our lives; good or bad was designed to not only make us stronger but make us wiser. Just because we've experienced pain doesn't give us the right to self-victimize or become professional victims. We are not Victims! Our environment shouldn't have to experience the trauma we didn't heal from. That's why it is necessary for us to acknowledge our internal struggles. Those feelings of shame, blame and hate are the results of some form of trauma. Some of us even identify ourselves by our hurt and grow accustomed to living a toxic life. We often gravitate toward the things that keep us broken. The pain must be dealt with and not swept under a rug. The longer we avoid dealing with it, the more intense it becomes. It crawls from under that rug stronger, with a much bigger appetite to cause more chaos and add more trauma to our lives. It is important for us to carefully review and understand the events which occurred during our travels. When we don't acknowledge our experiences and behaviors; we become familiar and comfortable with the same story lines but, different sceneries. These events become repetitive! (Repeatedly repeated) Yup, I said it! We find ourselves in the same situations over and over again. Repeating what we don't repair! We must take personal responsibility and own the fact that we are responsible for how we perceive our life's journey, it's dynamics, and what we're going to make of it! I promise you that beyond the Pain, beyond the blame, beyond the guilt, beyond the shame and beyond the darkness there is a beautiful light that shines within.

Excerpt from "Affirmations for Travelin' Light"

-Melissa Sue Griffith

He gives strength to the weary and increases the power of the weak.

Isaiah 40:29

How did you interpret this scripture and how did it make you feel?

_____

_____

_____

_____

_____

_____

I STOOD ON MY FAITH REPLACED MY FEAR NOW I'M SOARING

-FELICIA NICOLE

Be on your guard; stand firm in the faith; be courageous; be strong.

1 Corinthians 16:13

How did you interpret this scripture and how did it make you feel?

_____

_____

_____

_____

_____

_____

_____

And your life would be brighter than noonday, and darkness will become like morning.
Job 11: 17

How did you interpret this scripture and how did it make you feel?

_____

_____

_____

_____

_____

_____

_____

It's been said many times but to me it's simple and true. Don't give up because tomorrow could be the day things get a little better. Keep going!!!

-Ladeanna Webb

_____

_____

_____

_____

_____

_____

_____

_____

Count your blessings and be thankful every day. There are a million people who would trade places with you, problems and all.

-Atiyah Gaye

_____

_____

_____

_____

_____

_____

_____

Giving up is not an option. Failure is a part of the process because if you don't experience failure how will you know when you've authentically won.

-Juanita Nichelle Kilpatrick

_____

_____

_____

_____

_____

_____

_____

_____

It is always the toughest and roughest just before a breakthrough is about to happen.

This is a proven fact! So, I say hold on, it's all just a test, getting you ready to handle and appreciate the greatness that's about to unfold in your life.

-Lenora Asbury

_____

_____

_____

_____

_____

_____

_____

_____

There's always someone with a much worse situation than yours who is still fighting. Count your blessings and don't give up the fight.

-Monica Townsend

I always say that no one is perfect. We're always going to have problems in life. That's a part of growing into who we are meant to be. We just have to keep the faith, pray and leave it in God's hands.

-Ivette Miranda

_____

_____

_____

_____

_____

_____

_____

_____

Always believe in yourself, know that you can do anything you set your mind to. Stay humble, kind and chase your dreams. Make your moves in silence and let your success make the noise!

-Tammy Mancuso-Jackson

_____

_____

_____

_____

_____

_____

_____

The Love of LaLa

As a younger woman I always questioned my worth and value. I tended to focus more on my faults/imperfections instead of my blessings. Today however as a beautiful black Queen I realize that every lesson, I mean everything I went through to become the woman I am today was necessary. As an overweight young adult, I couldn't see beauty past what society showed me. It took me having positive people in my life to help inspire me, and to love me for me. I realized and accepted that we are all different but uniquely beautiful in our own way and now I embrace every curve, every roll, every scar, every single thing about me and my Beautifully Blessed life.

Remember you are irreplaceably you, and there can never be any substitutes to your beautiful black girl magic!!!!

-LaLa

_____

_____

_____

_____

_____

_____

A Word to My Younger Self

We often hear people talk about the importance of living in the moment and the different ways it is beneficial. It all sounds wonderful, especially the lower levels of stress/anxiety, but how exactly can we live in the present when out mind is constantly worrying about the past or planning for the future? It took me a long time understand the value of the moment. I would tell my younger self to embrace the moment and enjoy it. Stop worrying about tomorrow and take full advantage of the present. In addition to that, I'd tell myself not to ever cling to a person, place or organization. Instead attach yourself to a mission, a calling, a purpose. I learned that's how you keep your power and your peace.

-Jill Fairley

Advice from a Mentor

Advice I would give to young women to inspire them not to give up

1. Trust God
2. Be financially literate
3. Know your worth
4. Never let anyone tell you or believe that you can't be Successful!

-Vanessa Anderson-Miskit

_____

_____

_____

_____

_____

_____

A Gem from Crystal

Dear Crystal,

Here is some advice, where you are in life is okay. You don't have to lie to people about where you are in life right now or what you've been through. You'll meet people, and you will inspire them to hold on.

Save your money, I know you've never made money before, but trust me when I say it's better to have money for a rainy day, listen to me rainy days are coming. All the people that you are helping now won't be around to help you, they'll leave.

Love yourself, you're insecure because you don't love yourself, you don't see how beautiful and talented you are. One day you'll find your calling and it'll be up from there. Everyday wont a good day and that's okay.

Cry it out, get dressed extra pretty and press on. You'll have kids in the future don't worry you'll be a great mom. You're going to get married. I know right now you don't want to but trust me when I say this guy is different. He's a keeper and will love you with his whole heart. Him and your children will help you get through some storms, and you'll thank God for blessing you with them.

Trust the path God has you on. You're going to be okay. Stay close to God even when you don't feel him near, call on him he'll come. Staying close to God will protect you from what's to come. I love you, take care of yourself. Oh yeah, you will break generational curses of pain, lying and manipulation. It will take a lot of work; we will fall short from time to time but get up and keep going. Again, I love you beautiful lady.

-Crystal Jenkins

God is in control, never give up. God gives us life lessons that are supposed to build us up during our transition from our younger years into adulthood. These trials and tribulations are meant to make us into the people he has called us to be. Ever heard the saying, "God only gives us what we can handle or bare." This is true, in the end the message is to Never give up!

-Monique B

SELF CARE

Self-care is a necessary part of our mental, physical, emotional and spiritual well-being. It has been clinically proven to reduce or eliminate depression, anxiety and increases happiness in our lives. It is important that we take time daily for self-care. Although self-care practices are different for each person; meditating, listening to music or relaxing are just a few of many. Whatever it is, find what works for you and be consistent.

-Melissa Sue Griffith

What are your self-care practices?

_____

_____

_____

_____

_____

_____

BE STILL – BREATHE – RELAX - RELEASE

Today is the day I will:

_____

_____

_____

_____

_____

_____

_____

My last dream:

_____

_____

_____

_____

_____

_____

_____

_____

_____

What I won't Tolerate:

Today I found my why.

What is it?

_____

_____

_____

_____

_____

_____

_____

_____

_____

My Master Plan

My Circle: (Team)

_____

_____

_____

_____

_____

_____

_____

We are not meant to do things alone. Surround yourself with likeminded people that want to get to the next level. Remember though, this is your vision not theirs.

Mirror Mantra

Hi there pretty lady let me have a word with you

You are beautiful

You are capable

You can do or be anything you set your mind to

You are smart

This skin is gorgeous

These thighs are lovely

This body is just perfect, every curve, every stretchmark, every inch of me from

head to toe I love me, all of me

Now go shake the world girl

You got this shit!!!!!!!

-Felicia Nicole

Words from Wendy

Young ladies buckle up because it's gonna be one hell of a ride. This thing called life can kick your ass, you better kick back. Please remember to be gentle with yourself when you need to, but to also give yourself a kick in the ass when needed. You are your own cheerleader and life will get better.

-Wendy Creighton-Hunte

_____

_____

_____

_____

_____

_____

How to stay on track:

Plan:

Begin by writing down your goal or dream, be specific with the reasons WHY you're doing it.

_____

_____

_____

_____

_____

_____

_____

_____

By writing it down you are actively doing something to bring it to life rather than keeping it in your mind. BE realistic with yourself make the goal attainable.

Time Management:

Life can sometimes get in the way of our plans and that's okay. The key is carving out time to dedicate to your dream/goals. Use the calendar to work a schedule and time you want to commit to working on your goal/dream and no matter what stick to that time. Remember discipline is the key to success.

January	February	March	April
_____	_____	_____	_____
_____	_____	_____	_____
_____	_____	_____	_____
_____	_____	_____	_____
_____	_____	_____	_____

May	June	July	August
_____	_____	_____	_____
_____	_____	_____	_____
_____	_____	_____	_____
_____	_____	_____	_____

September	October	November	December
_____	_____	_____	_____
_____	_____	_____	_____
_____	_____	_____	_____
_____	_____	_____	_____

Monitor and record your successes and losses and adjust accordingly.

Celebrate all your victories and successes:

Don't forget to celebrate each victory no matter how small. There are no small victories, a win is a win!

List 7 things that deserve celebrating:

1. _____

2. _____

3. _____

4. _____

5. _____

6. _____

7. _____

CHEER FOR YOURSELF!!!!

THE PAIN OF YOUR JOURNEY WILL BE WORTH THE REWARD OF YOUR SUCCESS…

-FELICIA NICOLE

Choose your words and monitor your thoughts

Many of us are not aware of how powerful our mind and our words are.

If you think negative and speak negative the life you want cannot come to fruition.

Speak positively about yourself and your goals/dreams use words like, when I become a millionaire, or I will be a millionaire When I finish this project, or I will finish this project.

Believe it, speak it, and live it!

-Felicia Nicole

I AM:

_____

_____

_____

_____

_____

_____

_____

I WILL:

_____

_____

_____

_____

_____

_____

_____

Write a love letter to yourself:

_____

_____

_____

_____

_____

_____

_____

_____

_____

Welcome to your next Level

You've made the decision to take a step towards a greater version of you. You have decided to look inside, to get to know the woman that is you. It is not easy to face our fears, or to hold ourselves accountable. Often, we are comfortable in our discomfort. Thank you for choosing to move on to your next Level of growth, from the love you've given or lost, the next level to heal from the pain of your past, the next level to success, both personal and professional. It's Levels to every part of life. YOUR NEXT LEVEL DEPENDS ON YOU!

How did you perceive this Journal?

_____

_____

_____

_____

_____

_____

_____

_____

_____

_____

_____

_____

_____

_____

-You're almost there keep going….